SAFETY FIRST

Written By: Tracé Wilkins Francis
Illustrated by: HH-Pax

Annie Jean Publishing

The Real Life Adventures Of

Jo Jo Bean

Copyright © 2019, 2014 Tracé Wilkins Francis

ISBN 978-0-578-46881-5

Library of Congress Control Number: 2019902405

Printed in the U.S.A.

Annie Jean Publishing, Inc.
New York

www.anniejeanpublshing.com

Summary: Jo Jo Bean's granddad takes him to the new town pool where he learns about water safety.

Jo Jo Bean's granddad promised to take him to the new town pool on the first hot sunny day. Today was the day.

He was so excited that he ran out the door bumping into poor Granddad's stomach. Granddad let out a big sigh.

Before Jo Jo Bean knew it, he was standing in front of the coolest pool he had ever seen! He got dizzy as his eyes followed the yellow, red, and green slides that twisted and turned from the sky to the ground. The lounge chairs were perfectly lined up around the pool.

Jo Jo Bean looked by the edge of the pool and saw his best friends Twisty Tina and Worry Wendell. He ran towards them but was stopped by Sam the Lifeguard.

"Hold on there young fellow. No running at the pool!" warned Sam.

"Jo Jo Bean you could have fallen and hurt yourself!" said Twisty Tina.
"Or someone else like me!" said Worry Wendell.

Jo Jo Bean didn't want to hurt anyone else, especially his friends. "I promise I won't run anymore. I know! Let's go down the big red slide on our stomachs like Superman!"

"That's too dangerous! We could hurt ourselves," said Worry Wendell. "If you go down too fast on your stomach, you can hit your head against the pool wall!" said Twisty Tina.

"Your friends are right Jo Jo Bean!" He turned around to see Granddad standing over him. His face was the color of the tomatoes in his grandmother's garden.

"What did I say about the pool?" asked Granddad
"Uh, you would take me to the pool on the first hot sunny day?" asked Jo Jo Bean.
"I meant right before we left to come here," said Granddad.

Jo Jo Bean hoped his answer would stop the red smoke that was coming out of Granddad's ears. It only made it worse.

"Jo Jo Bean, I'm only going to say this one more time. No running, flipping, karate kicking, or Superman sliding while at this pool! Got it?" "Got it." Jo Jo Bean couldn't figure out how he was going to have any fun if he couldn't run, flip, karate kick, or superman slide. Twisty Tina put her hand on Jo Jo Bean's shoulder.

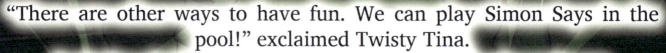

"There are other ways to have fun. We can play Simon Says in the pool!" exclaimed Twisty Tina.
Jo Jo Bean's face lit up like the brightest star in the universe.
"Can I be Simon first?"

His friends looked at each other and nodded their heads.

"Jo Jo Bean can we start now? My fingers are turning into raisins," said Worry Wendell.

Jo Jo Bean grinned and began the first round of Simon Says.

"SIMON SAYS jump on one foot!"
"SIMON SAYS do jumping jacks!"
"SIMON SAYS stop!"

Twisty Tina, Worry Wendell, and Granddad tried to stop him. "JO JO BEAN WAIT...NO!"

Jo Jo Bean didn't notice the other children playing in the water near him.
…Or the people sunbathing on the lounge chairs on the pool deck.
…Or the moms drying off their babies.
…Or the teenagers taking selfies with their cell phones.

Jo Jo Bean made the biggest splash anyone at the pool had ever seen.
"Look at what you did!" said Worry Wendell.
Jo Jo Bean looked around and saw:
Crying babies;
Soaked sunbathers;
Angry teenager; and
Upset mothers.

He hung his head low and began to cry.
"I didn't mean to make everyone upset. I was just having fun!"

He felt his Granddad's thumb wipe away the tears on his cheek.
"I know you didn't mean to do it, but you have to think about other people too."

Sam the Lifeguard walked over to Jo Jo Bean. "We have rules at the pool so everyone has fun in a safe way."

"You could fall and hurt yourself, even if you are skipping. The pool deck is very wet and slippery," said Worry Wendell.

"You also shouldn't make big splashes when people are nearby. It's not nice and quite rude," said Twisty Tina.

"You can still have fun while obeying the rules. Remember, safety first!" said Sam the Lifeguard.

"I'll remember." Jo Jo Bean thought for a few seconds and smiled.

"I have the greatest idea ever!"

"What is it?" everyone asked.
"From now on, I'm going to be a lifeguard to make sure everyone follows the pool rules! Captain Aqua Kid to the rescue!"

SAFETY FIRST POOL/BEACH TIPS

Nothing can top a fun-filled adventure at the pool, lake, beach, or water park. Whether you are outside on a hot sunny day or inside enjoying the slides at an indoor water park, please remember to follow some of these important rules:

- Listen and follow the directions of the lifeguard on duty.

- Do not run near the pool area.

- Never go through any pool gates at someone's house when the gates are closed.

- Always obey the rules posted at the pool, lake, beach or water park.

- Always go down the water slide face up and feet first. This is the safe and correct way to slide.

- Exit immediately after you reach the bottom of a water slide. You don't want the next slider bumping into you.

- Do not chew or eat while playing or swimming in the water. You can choke.

- Avoid swallowing water.

- Wear a coast guard approved life jacket, especially if you are learning how to swim.

- When at the beach, always face the ocean so you can see when a big wave is coming.

- Never wander off by yourself. Make sure there is always an adult watching you.

BOOKS IN THE REAL LIFE ADVENTURES OF JO JO BEAN SERIES

Birthday Bubbles

Delectable Vegetables

Safety First

COMING SOON

The Christmas Coat

Park Blues

If you are interested in purchasing this series for your classroom, school, or day care, please email *anniejeanpublishing@gmail.com*. We also do author visits with the characters.

eaf7bd35-007a-4b55-8110-0f154cfc751aR01